I'm Sorry . . . My Bad!

Other Books by Bradley Trevor Greive

The Blue Day Book*

The Blue Day Journal and Directory

Dear Mom*

Looking for Mr. Right

The Meaning of Life

The Incredible Truth About Mothers

Tomorrow

Priceless: The Vanishing Beauty of a Fragile Planet

The Book for People Who Do Too Much

Friends to the End*

Dear Dad*

The Simple Truth About Love

A Teaspoon of Courage

Dieting Causes Brain Damage

Every Day Is Christmas

Thank You for Being You

For Children

The Blue Day Book for Kids

Friends to the End for Kids

A Teaspoon of Courage for Kids

*Available in Spanish

I'm Sorry... My Bad!

BRADLEY TREVOR GREIVE

**Andrews McMeel
Publishing, LLC**

Kansas City

ISBN-13: 978-0-7407-7380-8
ISBN-10: 0-7407-7380-1

Library of Congress Control Number: 2008922540

08 09 10 11 12 TWP 10 9 8 7 6 5 4 3 2 1

www.andrewsmcmeel.com

Attention: Schools and Businesses

Andrews McMeel books are available at quantity discounts with bulk purchase for educational, business, or sales promotional use. For information, please write to: Special Sales Department, Andrews McMeel Publishing, LLC, 1130 Walnut Street, Kansas City, Missouri 64106.

For everyone I have offended
or hope to offend at some later date.

ACKNOWLEDGMENTS

It seems apt that *I'm Sorry . . . My Bad* begins with an apology for my nostalgic indulgence. You are not obliged to wallow with me, so please feel free to skip to the book proper, which begins a few pages to your right.

Looking back to the debut of *The Blue Day Book*, at the end of last century, I never cease to be amazed that, after my years of heroic failure, it was a small, grumpy blue frog that finally got my literary career off the ground. As a wry celebration of human frailty, I suppose Proustian comparisons are inevitable. However, apart from a shared penchant for chunky knitwear, unkempt beards, and brightly colored drinks, I make no claim to be Hemingway writ small. But if you have enjoyed reading my little books even half as much as I have enjoyed writing them, then I must confess a bone-deep buzz of happy satisfaction well beyond anything I should ever legally be entitled to.

If this is our last time together then it seems, above all, to be an ideal opportunity to say sorry. If my humorous gift books have brought you pleasure over the years, then I apologize that this series has come to an end. And if they did not please you, then I am sorry this series has gone on for as long as it has.

I apologize to the team at BTG Studios and my publishing family throughout the world for not making you all more aware of just how important you are to me and how grateful I am for your friendship, support, and inspiration.

To the photographers and their agents who have shared their premium photographs with me, I deeply regret that so few of your splendid images could be published.

If unchecked, I would—now that the spirit of contrition is upon me—apologize to everyone I have ever met, but time and space moves against me. So instead I will simply say to those whom, I have disappointed, wounded, or laid low over the years, I am sincerely sorry. Please believe this was the opposite of my intention.

If there is one person to whom I am truly in rueful arrears, it is my magnanimous mentor and international literary agent, the legendary Sir Albert J. Zuckerman of Writers House, New York.

Like so many aspiring authors, I thought I already knew everything when I started. No amount of professional instruction or friendly advice seemed to make it past my cauliflower ears.

When Al graciously accepted me into the venerated Writers House stable, he was incredibly patient. After a few false starts, he decided the best way to teach me the virtues of humility and hard work was by pairing me up with leading authors he represented so that I might observe and learn from them. I was a terrible student.

To this day I'm still embarrassed that a heated audience with scientific supremo Stephen Hawking ended with the parting shot, "Yeah, well, you talk funny!" Things didn't go much better with Nora Roberts, Ken Follett, Tim Willocks, Barbara Delinsky, Michael Lewis, Erica Jong, Neil Gaiman, or Janet Evanovich. Sharon Creech sicced her dog onto me and when, after four hours of shouting, the kindly and learned representative from the estate of Martin Luther King got fed up and suggested we "take it outside," Al knew he had to step in.

Tough love was the key. Al's own father had taught him how to box in the basement of their apartment building in the Cloisters in northern Manhattan, not far from the NYU tennis facility where Al now competes every winter. The pugilistic workouts got harder and faster until one day, a week or so before Al's tenth birthday, he laid his old man out cold with a devastating three-punch combination he called "Giraudoux's Curtain Call." After that, they started playing Ping-Pong.

When I arrived at 21 West Twenty-second Street, Al would take me into the safe room at the back of the Writers House brownstone and, using an egg timer to keep track of the rounds, we would go at it all day. Al peppered my stubborn jowls with lightning jabs and worked my soft midsection with both fists, all the while bombarding me with lessons on exposition, dramatic arc, grammar, narrative scope, setting, authentic voice, and even authorial dress and bearing. Al never seemed to tire, and each night I collapsed onto my bed like a boneless walrus and sobbed softly into my pillow, which Al had thoughtfully stuffed with both volumes of the *Shorter Oxford English Dictionary* to keep my dreams focused.

This went on for some time until one day, I insisted Al order an extra dessert following a sumptuous meal at Eleven Madison Park, our usual luncheon venue. Thus, when we put the gloves back on thirty minutes later, Al was suitably slowed by the effects of postprandial torpor, and I ruffled his noble mustache with a cheeky right hook. Then, while he was still stunned, I rushed in close and rattled off the subtle distinction between "farther" and "further." I then flopped to the canvas beside him, and we sat there for a moment staring at each other in mute astonishment. Al dusted himself off, smiled warmly after helping me to my feet, and announced I was ready to start my literary apprenticeship.

The following weekend, Al asked me to come into Writers House to help him tidy up his office. This was no small feat as, over the decades, manuscripts from celebrated authors had piled up to create a literary eclipse across both doors and most of the windows. Bringing order to this luminous chaos was slow going. Not only were the stacks so precarious and heavy that I felt my vertebrae creaking in complaint whenever I tried to shift them, but we would often stumble across writing that was so incredibly good we were both forced to pause, sometimes mid-lift, to admire an exquisite sentence, a bracing paragraph, or even an extraordinary chapter or two.

Stopping only to refuel on Zabar's high-octane coffee, we toiled long into the night. Finally, just after 1 a.m., crumpled and sweaty with fatigue, Al and I dusted off the final shelf and placed the last treasured volumes carefully into their proper order. Then we shuffled back down Eighth Avenue to Chelsea, too tired to speak.

When we reached the steps to the Zuckerman home, Al thanked me for my labors, stretched his aching back, then straightened to give me a good-night bear hug. Turning back from the doorway, he looked at me fondly and said, "Bradley, my boy, I'm just sorry that we can't do this till the end of time."

I'm sorry too, Al. I really am.

Wait. Please don't turn away. Just hear me out—that's all I ask.

It's all my fault, and I am so sorry.

I know I was wrong, but it still isn't easy to come clean.

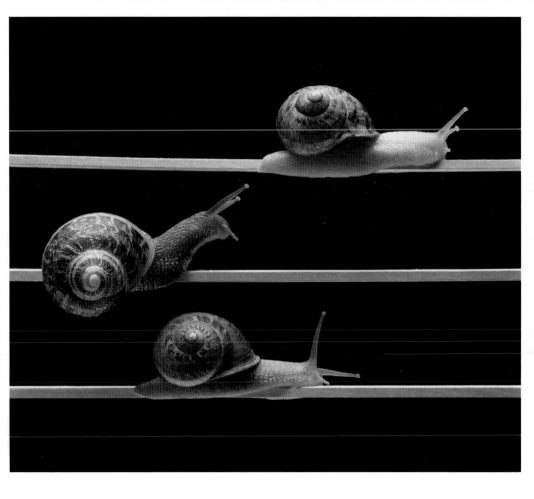

I've wanted to apologize for what seems an eternity,
but it's taken awhile for me to summon up the
necessary courage and the right words.

The longer I waited, the harder it was to talk to you,

and now, at the moment of truth, I collapse into a tongue-tied,
emotional wreck capable only of meaningless Yoda-speak.
Though amusing, from time to time, this is, yes.

So, with one last deep breath through the nose,
I enter my "happy place." My heartbeat is steady. I am calm.
Let me start by saying I am sorry I screwed up.

I mean, I really screwed up big time, and boy, do I know it! 17

What I did was so thoughtless—
worse than eating the center out of all the Oreo cookies in the world,

even worse than secretly peeing in a hot tub.

And talk about stupid. What I did was even dumber than buying ludicrous exercise equipment from a cheesy midnight TV infomercial

or pretending to be a gangsta rapper to look cool.

21

It's all my fault there is a weird barrier between us now. I blew it.

I pushed you too far,

broke your heart,

made you mad,

and turned your world on its head.

I feel sick knowing that if you were a lesser being,
you might even have turned to strong drink,

questioned the foundations of your faith,

or perhaps written some really lousy and depressing poetry
that would have brought everyone else down, too.

Question:
Who's the biggest, stupidest jerk in the known universe?

Answer:
Me.

I'm also stubborn,

smug,

and just plain rude.

Did I mention I was also a lazy, smelly slob,

a pathetic whiner,

a pious twit,

and a big fat quitter who let you down?

I should have known better, and I am deeply ashamed of myself.

"D'oh!" Why oh why did I do it? What a loser!
How could I have been so stupid?!

My guilt is so profound and my regret so intense
that it makes my teeth ache.

I don't know why you should care, but there is only one way
for me to be free of this torment, and that is if you will accept
my full and sincere apology.

No matter what happens between us,
I just want you to know how truly sorry I am.

43

44   **Nothing makes me sadder than seeing how sad I have made you.**

Please open your heart and let me back into your good graces.

46   I promise I can and will make it up to you. You won't regret it.

I swear I will never do anything bad as long as I live.
Cross my heart and hope to die.

May God, in his infinite wisdom, afflict my tender buttocks with ten thousand explosive boils for all eternity if I ever upset you again.

I'm on my knees here, begging you to accept my apology.

I am on my belly, crawling toward you
with my lips, pleading for forgiveness.

You have every reason to be upset with me,

**and you are fully entitled to wash your hands of me
once and for all.**

Even the angel on your shoulder must be telling you to
close your ears, avert your eyes, and walk away—but please ignore her,
just this one time. I beseech you.

53

If you give me one more chance I shall zip my lip
and never ever ask for anything else for the rest of my life.

So, what do you say? Can we start again? Can we, please?

Sure, it might be awkward and clunky for a little while,

but I believe we can get our rhythm back before you know it.

We just need some quality time together
to rebuild the trust I damaged,

and eventually it could be just like old times—who knows?
Maybe even better . . .

In a nutshell, what I want to say is this:
"I'm truly, deeply, and genuinely sorry for everything!"

Can we be friends again?

Please?

Photo Credits

Age Fotostock • www.agefotostock.com

Corbis Australia PTY Ltd • www.corbis.com

Emerald City Images • www.emeraldcityimages.com.au

Fairfax Photos • www.Fairfaxphotos.com

Getty Images • www.gettyimages.com

Jupiter Images • www.jupiterimages.com.au

Daniel J. Cox/Natural Exposures • www.naturalexposures.com

Naturepl.com • www.naturepl.com

Photolibrary • www.photolibrary.com

© Steve Bloom • www.stevebloom.com

Wildlight Photo Agency • www.wildlight.net

Detailed page credits for the remarkable photographers whose work appears in *I'm Sorry . . . My Bad!* and other books by Bradley Trevor Greive are freely available at www.btg.studios.com.